LIVING GREEN

Mountains, Deserts, and Grasslands

WORLD BOOK

a Scott Fetzer company

Chicago

www.worldbookonline.com

Editorial:

Editor in Chief: Paul A. Kobasa
Project Manager: Cassie Mayer
Writer: Edward R. Ricciuti
Editor: Daniel Kenis
Researchers: Daniel Kenis, Jacqueline Jasek
Manager, Contracts & Compliance
  (Rights & Permissions): Loranne K. Shields
Indexer: David Pofelski

Graphics and Design:

Manager: Tom Evans
Coordinator, Design Development
  and Production: Brenda B. Tropinski
Book design by: Don Di Sante
Senior Designer: Isaiah W. Sheppard, Jr.
Contributing Photographs Editor: Carol Parden
Senior Cartographer: John Rejba

Pre-Press and Manufacturing:

Director: Carma Fazio
Manufacturing Manager: Steve Hueppchen
Production/Technology Manager: Anne Fritzinger

World Book, Inc.
233 N. Michigan Avenue
Chicago, IL 60601
U.S.A.

For information about other World Book publications, visit our Web site at **http://www.worldbookonline.com** or call **1-800-WORLDBK (967-5325).**

For information about sales to schools and libraries, call **1-800-975-3250 (United States)**, or **1-800-837-5365 (Canada).**

Picture Acknowledgments:

Cover: © Josef Beck, Imagebroker/Alamy

© AfriPics/Alamy 27, 49; © Alaska Stock/Alamy 15; © Arco Images GmbH/Alamy 47, 50; © Jon Arnold Images/Alamy 26; © Trevor Smithers, ARPS/Alamy 39; © Bill Bachman, Alamy 57; © Krys Bailey, Alamy 24; © blickwinkel/Alamy 38; © Mark Boulton, Alamy 51; © Shaughn F. Clements, Alamy 48; © Richard Cooke, Alamy 49; © Chris Cheadle, Alamy 54; © JupiterImages/Creatas/Alamy 58; © Ian Dagnall, Alamy 19; © Danita Delimont, Alamy 20; © Michael Dwyer, Alamy 11; © Pavel Filatov, Alamy 8; © David R. Frazier Photolibrary/Alamy 30; © Fred Grover Jr., Alamy 23; © Thomas Hallstein, Alamy 29; © Robert Harding Picture Library/Alamy 37, 55; © Jim Havey, Alamy 13, 53; © Image State/Alamy 5; © Images&Stories/Alamy 41; © IMAGINA Photography/Alamy 27; © Israel Images/Alamy Image 32; © Jacques Jangoux, Alamy 13; © Mark A. Johnson, Alamy 18; © Juniors Bildarchiv/Alamy 22; © Wolfgang Kaehler, Alamy 42; © Kuttig-Travel/Alamy 45; © Lighthouse Imaging/Alamy 31; © Mcmaster Studio/Alamy 48; © McPhoto/Alamy 15; © Charles Mistral, Alamy 12; © Galen Rowell, Mountain Light/Alamy 14; © Ron Niebrugge, Alamy 36; © David Noble Photography/Alamy 29; © M. Timothy O'Keefe, Alamy 52; © Douglas Peebles Photography/Alamy 34; © RWP, Alamy 47; © David Sanger Photography/Alamy 10; © Kevin Schafer, Alamy 32; © Martin Shields, Alamy 9; © Michael Snell, Alamy 45; © David South, Alamy 17; © Stock Connection Distribution/Alamy 23; © John Sylvester, Alamy 4, 44; © Bob Turner, Alamy 16; © Genevieve Vallee, Alamy 40; © Greg Vaughn, Alamy 6; © Worldwide Picture Library/Alamy 46; © Marek Zuk, Alamy 28; © Gary Braasch 21; © AFP/Getty Images 56; © Erin Patrice O'Brien, Getty Images 58; © Fred Greaves, Bloomberg News/Landov 35; © Craig K. Lorenz, Photo Researchers 33; H. Slupetzky, University of Salzburg 21; © Thomas R. Van Devender 39; © Paul Elkan, Wildlife Conservation Society 51.

All maps and illustrations are the exclusive property of World Book, Inc.

The Library of Congress has cataloged an earlier edition of this title as follows:

Mountains, deserts, and grasslands.
   p. cm. -- (Living green)
   Includes index.
   Summary: "General overview of mountain, desert, and grassland ecosystems, including an exploration of disturbances these ecosystems face due to human interference and climate change; and current conservation and reclamation efforts. Features include fact boxes, sidebars, activities, glossary, list of recommended reading and Web sites, and index"--Provided by publisher.
   ISBN 978-0-7166-1403-6
   1. Mountains--Juvenile literature. 2. Deserts--Juvenile literature. 3. Grasslands--Juvenile literature. I. World Book, Inc.
GB512M68 2009
333.95'16--dc22
                          2008032216

This edition:
ISBN: 978-0-7166-1413-5
ISBN: 978-0-7166-1410-4 (set)
Printed in China by:
Leo Paper Products LTD.,
Heshan, Guangdong
3rd Printing April 2010

The pages inside this book are printed with a waterless printing process that eliminates volatile organic compounds (VOC's) from the printing process. Some VOC's have been linked to the deterioration of Earth's protective ozone layer and, consequently, to global warming. For more information on waterless printing, go to www.waterless.org.

Waterless
Printing. Nature

Table of Contents

There is a glossary of terms on pages 60-61. Terms defined in the glossary are in type **that looks like this** on their first appearance in any section.

Introduction

Section Summary

Mountains, deserts, and grasslands are ecosystems that each have their own unique climate, vegetation, and animal life. However, these ecosystems are also closely connected. Mountains often border deserts, with grasslands growing within mountain ranges. Mountains also shape the climate of deserts and grasslands nearby.

Human activities have damaged these ecosystems. For example, some areas have been cleared to develop land for farming, housing, or recreation. Global warming, believed by most scientists to be caused by human activities, is a major threat to these ecosystems.

Towering mountains, windswept deserts, and lush grasslands are all unique environments. Human beings have built huge farms and cities on grasslands. On the other hand, mountains and deserts have usually been barriers for human civilization. Only a few communities of people call deserts their home, and nobody lives on the highest mountains.

Mountains rise above rolling grasslands in Canada's Yukon.

It is hard to imagine how an icy mountain peak is linked to a blazing hot desert or a cool, flat stretch of **prairie.** But in spite of their differences, these three environments are often closely connected. Mountain ranges can rise from deserts, with grasslands growing on plateaus and valleys within the range. In some places, such as the areas surrounding the Black Hills of South Dakota, grassland meets the mountain slopes.

Mountains also shape the climate conditions that give rise to deserts and grasslands nearby. Mountain ranges are like walls that block the flow of moist air as it moves over land. As the air rises over mountains, it drops its moisture in the form of rain and snow. The air that eventually makes its way over the mountains is dry. Deserts often form behind mountain ranges where little rain falls.

The amount of **precipitation** in an area determines what kind of plants can grow there. Deserts have the least precipitation, and the least amount of life. They are often bordered by dry grasslands, and wetter grasslands often border forests. Much of the water flowing through and under deserts and grasslands often comes from melting snow and ice that flows down mountains.

Environmental change

Changes in the environment, whether caused by nature or people, can have tremendous impact on mountains, deserts, and grasslands. A good example is what happens when vegetation is removed. It makes no difference whether the vegetation is in the form of trees on a mountain slope, grasses on a plain, or low, thorny desert plants. Once stripped of vegetation, the soil is vulnerable to **erosion** by wind and water. Soil can be carried down mountain slopes, leaving them almost bare and polluting waterways below. Once topsoil is blown or washed away from grasslands, they lose their rich **fertility.** Plants hold the sand of desert dunes in place. Without vegetation, the wind can destroy dunes and the community of plants and animals that live within them.

Mountains block the flow of precipitation to such desert areas as Death Valley in California.

What Are Mountains?

Section Summary

Mountains are pieces of earth that rise above the surrounding land. Mountains shape the climate of regions around them.

Many human activities have damaged mountain habitats. For example, forests are often cleared for wood or to make room for farming, housing developments, and recreational activities.

Global warming is changing mountain environments. Plants and animals that live in cooler temperatures could be forced to higher slopes or even vanish if their surroundings become too warm.

In the simplest terms, a mountain is a landform, a feature of Earth's surface, which rises much higher than the surrounding terrain, or landscape.

Volcanic mountains, such as Mount Saint Helens, form from molten rock beneath Earth's surface.

This description could also fit a hill, although mountains are generally thought of as larger than hills.

Major mountain ranges can influence climate far beyond their boundaries. Ranges such as these include the Rocky Mountains, the Sierra Nevada, and the Pacific System in North America; the Andes Mountains of South America; the Himalaya of southern Asia; and the Alps of Europe.

Volcanic mountains

Mountains arise from powerful forces beneath Earth's crust. Mountains are classified into two types, according to the way they were formed. Volcanic mountains, which make up one type, form from **molten** rock deep within Earth that makes its way to the surface. When the molten rock is underground, it is known as **magma**. When it erupts above ground, it is called **lava**.

Above the surface, lava cools and eventually builds up into a type of mountain known as a volcano. Mount Fuji in Japan and Hawaii's Mauna Loa are examples of large, spectacular volcanoes. Approximately 600 of Earth's 10,000 volcanoes are active, meaning that they still erupt on occasion.

Tectonic mountains

Tectonic mountains get their name from the theory of **plate tectonics**. According to this theory, Earth's outer shell is made of about 30 pieces, called tectonic plates, which fit together like a jigsaw puzzle. The plates continuously move, and sometimes they smash into each other or scrape over and under one another, forming tectonic mountains.

There are four types of tectonic mountains. Fold-thrust mountains occur when two plates collide. The crust folds upward, like a rumpled tablecloth, and some layers of rock may be thrust over other layers. The Alps of Europe, the Rockies and Appalachian Mountains of the United States, and the Himalaya of southern Asia were built this way.

Fault-block mountains form when plates drift away from one another. Gaps, called **faults** or rifts, separate them. The rock walls towering above the faults are pushed up, often tilted, to form mountains. The Sierra Nevada in the United States and the Black Forest of Germany are fault-block mountains.

Dome mountains form when geological forces lift up Earth's crust into a bulging shape. Erosion mountains form when soft rock is worn away, leaving harder rock exposed.

Mountain ranges influence a variety of human activities, shaping patterns of transportation, communication, and settlement.

The Gobi is a desert that lies in the "rain shadow" on the leeward side of the Himalaya in Mongolia.

MOUNTAINS' INFLUENCE ON WEATHER AND CLIMATE

Mountains are often described as weather-makers. Mountain ranges can shape the climate of regions around them because they block the flow of air, forcing it to move upward. At higher **altitudes**, the air's pressure decreases, and air absorbs less heat. Cold air cannot hold as much moisture as warmer air. When moist air blows against a mountain range and becomes cooler, its moisture **condenses**, turning from a gas to a liquid, and falls to the ground as **precipitation.**

Because of the way mountains affect air, two sides of a mountain range may have extremely different climates. The **windward** side of a mountain range—that is, the side that faces the blowing winds—is usually wetter than the **leeward** side.

Rain shadows

Air that reaches a mountain's leeward side is already dry. As the air passes down the leeward slope, it warms, losing even more moisture. The region around a mountain's leeward side is called a **rain shadow.** Many deserts are in rain shadows.

Rain shadows often contrast with the wetter, forested windward side of the same mountain range. For example, the Sierra Nevada has great forests on its western windward slopes, which receive several feet of snow in winter. But deserts lie on the eastern leeward side of the same mountain range, including bone-dry Death Valley.

In South America, the eastern windward slopes of the central Andes Mountains are heavily forested and well watered. As the mountains rise, the forest becomes so rain-soaked that it is cloaked in mist and clouds. It is often called a **cloud forest.** Above the cloud forest is a vast plateau, called the **Altiplano.** Only a small amount of rain makes it to the Altiplano, which is cold, windswept, and treeless. Most of the landscape is covered with low bunchgrass and sedges (grasslike plants that grow in wet places).

The leeward slopes that descend from the Altiplano to the Pacific Ocean are rocky, sandy, and dry, with little vegetation. Below these slopes, in the rain shadow of the Andes, lie deserts that stretch to the shores of the ocean in some areas. Part of this region is the Atacama Desert, the driest place on Earth. Some parts of this desert have had no rain for centuries.

Moisture cloaks the slopes of Costa Rica's Tilaran range, creating a "cloud forest."

Water storage

The large amount of precipitation that falls on mountains makes them important stores of fresh water. Where the climate is cold enough, much of this water is frozen into glaciers. Water melting from the edges of the glaciers forms the source of many rivers that bring moisture to lands below. Many of the world's great rivers originate in mountains. The Ganges River of the Indian subcontinent, the Amazon of South America, and the Yangtze of China all begin in mountain glaciers.

MOUNTAIN CLIMATES

The climate atop a mountain is often very different from that of the lowlands below. The climate may change rapidly as one moves up the slope of a mountain. In fact, geologists often define mountains as areas that include two or more climate zones. In most parts of the world, a mountain must rise about 2,000 feet (600 meters) to include two climate zones.

All mountains get colder toward their peaks. However, the closer a mountain is to the equator, the warmer its slopes are. The climate is warm enough in the Andes Mountains of tropical Bolivia for trees to grow up to about 13,000 feet (4,000 meters). But in Chile, at the southern tip of South America, the climate is so cold that trees can only grow on the lowest slopes of the Andes.

Worlds apart

Only low-growing plants, such as shrubs and moss, can survive on high mountain slopes.

Even in the tropics, the climate atop high mountains is worlds apart from the land below. Mount Kenya in East Africa is 17,058 feet (5,199 meters) high. It stands in tropical **savanna**, plains that now are mostly farmed. At about 9,800 feet (3,000 meters), trees are almost gone and the temperature is as cool as early spring in much of North America. At 14,763 feet (4,500 meters), vegetation dwindles to nothing. Bare rock and glaciers mark the landscape. Although the mountain is located only a few miles north of the equator, the climate on its **summit** is like that of the Arctic.

Not far from Mount Kenya lie the Aberdare Mountains. They are about 13,000 feet (4,000 meters) high. Although some vegetation grows on their peaks, the climate there is too cold for trees.

Wild weather

A mountain does not have to be among the world's highest places to have fierce weather near its summit. Mount Washington in New Hampshire is only 6,288 feet (1,917 meters) in altitude. But even though Mount Washington is located in **temperate** New England, it has some of the wildest weather on Earth.

Mount Washington's weather results from a combination of its **latitude**, altitude, and winds that cause several storm tracks to meet nearby. The fastest wind ever recorded—231 miles (372 kilometers) an hour—swept Mount Washington on April 12, 1943. Hurricane-force winds can occur there in any month of the year and do so on more than 100 days annually. The summer temperature on its peak has never been recorded above the low 70's °F (low 20's °C). Even when temperatures are at summer highs in the New Hampshire countryside below the mountain, snow can fall on its peak. Winter temperatures have dropped to about –50 °F (–45.5 °C) on the mountain.

Despite the region's temperate climate, the weather on New Hampshire's Mount Washington is often fierce.

MOUNTAIN PLANTS

Life on mountains is grouped in a series of zones from bottom to top. Each zone is marked by the kinds of plants growing there. The kinds of plants that grow on a mountain are determined by the location of the mountain. The varieties of plants that grow in a zone, in turn, determine what animals inhabit it.

Up to the timber line

Hiking up a high mountain takes a traveler through many different **habitats**. The lower slopes of the Rocky Mountains, for example, may rise from grasslands, especially on their eastern side. In some areas, woodlands of cottonwood and alder trees grow along streams. Higher up the slope, at an altitude between 4,900 and 8,000 feet (1,500 and 2,440 meters), patches of blue grama grass grow among scattered woodlands of juniper trees and piñon pine. These plants are found in the **foothills zone** of the Rocky Mountains.

From 8,000 to 10,000 feet (2,440 to 3,050 meters) in the Rockies, the high country of the **montane zone** begins. Forests of coniferous (cone-bearing) trees, such as ponderosa pine, Douglas-fir, and lodgepole pine, grow in the montane zone. Bearberry is a common low plant, and small oak trees are scattered about.

Farther up, from 10,000 to 12,000 feet (3,050 to 3,660 meters), lies the **subalpine zone** of the Rockies. The climate here is like in the forests of northern Canada. Among the trees are Engelmann spruce, aspen, and subalpine fir.

Above the timber line

Above 12,000 feet (3,660 meters), the **alpine zone** begins. This zone is above the timber line, where cold and wind prevent trees from growing. Where the subalpine and alpine zones meet, a few trees manage to keep a foothold. Trees that would grow to towering heights on lower slopes are stunted near the alpine zone,

The plant life on mountain slopes changes depending on the altitude, eventually fading away at the timber line.

only growing a few feet high at most. This type of growth is called *krummholz,* which means "crooked wood."

The plants of the alpine zone are like those of the Arctic **tundra.** They have **adaptations** that help them survive powerful wind and chilling cold. Many plants, such as the alpine anemone (*uh NEHM uh nee*), grow only a few inches high. By keeping low, they avoid being blown over by the wind. They also stay small because they grow slowly. The growing season is short in the alpine zone, so plants remain **dormant** in winter.

Soil in the alpine zone is thin, so many plants grow with spreading, shallow roots that cover as much ground as possible in the search for nutrients. Leathery or hairy leaves insulate them from the cold and protect them from the wind.

Eventually, as altitude increases, even small plants disappear. All that remains are small patches of mosses and **lichens,** plant-like organisms that are actually combinations of algae and fungi living together.

On the highest mountain peaks, plant life vanishes completely. The highest mountain slopes are zones of rock, bare or covered with snow and the ice of glaciers. These areas are similar to the barren, icy realms in the harshest parts of the Arctic and Antarctic.

Mountain trees, such as bristlecone pines, are specially adapted to the harsh, cold, windy conditions of high slopes.

A CLOSER LOOK
Mountaintop Habitats

Life atop mountains is often isolated from surrounding regions. Mountains are home to plants and animals that are specially adapted to conditions there and are cut off from the rest of the world. Some mountain plants and animals cannot live anywhere else.

Botanists estimate that 75 percent of plants growing in the Guiana Highlands of Venezuela are found nowhere else on Earth. A tiny mole shrew that lives near the top of Mount Kenya does not live anywhere else in the world. The Haleakala volcano on the Hawaiian island of Maui is the home of a giant tree geranium that lives only there.

Venezuela's Guiana Highlands

Mountain goats have special hoofs that allow them to cling to mountain cliffs.

MOUNTAIN ANIMALS

Many animals that live on the lower slopes of mountains are no different from those of surrounding lowlands. Pronghorns, adapted to plains life, range up into the foothills of the Rocky Mountains. White-tailed deer inhabit both lowland forests and the mountains of the eastern United States, which are not as high as many mountains west of the Mississippi River. The bodies and behavior of animals that live on the upper zones of high mountains, however, are specially adapted to life on cold, rocky slopes.

Physical adaptations

Several types of large, hoofed animals inhabit mountains in different parts of the world. Among them are wild sheep, such as the bighorn of North America, which lives in the subalpine zone of the Rocky Mountains. The bighorn has an undercoat of thick fleece. Above the fleece are hairs that are hollow inside that help insulate it against the cold. The Rocky Mountain goat—not a true goat but a member of a group called goat-antelopes—climbs even higher than the bighorn. It has a thick double coat that is extremely warm. The goat's Eurasian relative, the chamois (*SHAM ee*), has a similar coat.

The feet of the bighorn sheep, the chamois, and the mountain goat are adapted to climbing and jumping over steep, bare rock. The sole of the sheep's foot is cushioned, helping it move quickly on hard surfaces. The two-toed hoofs of mountain goats are flexible. The two halves of the foot can move independently, allowing them to fit into cracks in the rocks. The edges of the hoof are thin and hard, another way to grab on to cracks and crevices. In the center of the hoof, the goat has an elastic pad than acts like a tire tread.

The llama of South America also has padded feet that help it move around in the heights of the Andes Mountains. Llamas have an additional adaptation that helps them survive in the thin, oxygen-poor air near the Andes peaks: They have more red blood cells than most animals. These are the cells that pick up oxygen for breathing. The extra cells help the llama make up for the lower amount of oxygen available in its mountain home.

Behavioral adaptations

Just as some animals move north and south with the seasons, some mountain animals may move up the slope in summer and down the slope in winter. The North American elk finds better food in high pastures during summer but then moves into sheltered valleys for winter. Grizzly bears follow elk and other prey on seasonal migrations up and down the slopes.

In the mountains of Central Asia, the snow leopard, which lives at elevations up to 19,700 feet (6,000 meters) in summer, descends to less than half that altitude in winter. During summer, it hunts mountain sheep on the high peaks. Its winter prey consists of deer and smaller animals, such as rodents.

Rodents and other small animals are not able to make long journeys up and down the mountainside. Instead, they retreat into sheltered holes called burrows. During the coldest part of winter, many of them hibernate. In spring, they emerge from their burrows and resume their regular activities.

Grizzly bears move up and down mountains, tracking their seasonal prey.

People have lived in mountains since prehistoric times. The Native American peoples of the high Andes have lived in their mountain homes for many thousands of years. Others, such as the Sherpas of Nepal, may have moved into their mountain homes only a few centuries ago.

Humans cannot live on the very highest mountain peaks. However, foothills and even plateaus at high altitudes support large human populations. According to some estimates, about 12 percent of the world's population inhabits mountainous areas. Such populations are especially large in parts of Mexico and China.

Quechua people of the Andes

Mining can devastate mountain environments, leaving the topsoil bare.

INDUSTRIAL DEVELOPMENT

Mountains are often thought of as powerful and changeless. It is difficult to believe that people could do anything to damage them. Yet many scientists believe that of all **ecosystems**—communities of living things and their connected environment—those of mountains are among the most fragile. The steepness of mountain slopes puts them at risk from **erosion** by water and wind. Rugged and exposed to harsh weather, mountains are difficult places for plants and animals to live. Any additional disturbances of mountain environments by humans can tip the balance against the living things there.

Mountains are the scenes of human activity on an ever-increasing scale. Many of these activities are necessary for human welfare. However, some threaten to harm both people and natural ecosystems.

Infrastructure

Industries can damage mountain environments if they are not **regulated.** Such industries include logging, mining, and energy development. The activities themselves may harm mountains, but so can the development of **infrastructure** that comes with the industries. Miners and loggers need such infrastructure as roads, railways, housing, and other facilities to work and live. These structures can cause significant damage to mountain areas.

Mining

Among the mining techniques that worry **environmentalists** most is a method called **mountaintop removal.** Begun during the 1970's in the Appalachian Mountains, mountaintop removal blasts away entire tops of mountains to expose coal. Blasting comes after all trees and topsoil have been removed. The waste from blasting and digging fills valleys and often pollutes streams. Environmentalists say this process is much too destructive and that efforts to restore land after mining amount to little more than spreading grass seed over wasteland.

Logging

Clearcutting is a logging method that is often cited by environmentalists as extremely harmful to mountains. It is a cheap way to log because entire forests are simply leveled. An alternative method, in which only certain trees are selected for cutting and the remainder left alone, is more time-consuming and expensive. Eventually, new trees can be planted on clearcut land. Often, however, these are plantations of single tree species (called **monocultures**), not the varied vegetation of the original forest.

Besides destroying habitats, clearcutting has a severe impact on the land, both in the mountains and down below. Water runs quickly off clearcut land, so it is not stored for future use. Without vegetation to slow its movement down the slopes, water can cause erosion, sweeping away topsoil, stripping mountainsides, and filling streams below with **silt.**

Power plants

Many **hydroelectric** projects—dams and power plants that produce electric power—are built on mountain rivers. Though often considered essential to power homes and industries in the lowlands, dams can cause considerable environmental damage. For example, dams can affect the way in which rivers carry silt, or they can entirely redirect rivers.

While developed countries are moving toward stricter regulation of mountain industries, logging, mining, and similar activities are increasing in less developed countries. People in these areas are caught between needing the natural resources of mountains for their survival and trying to preserve the environment for the future.

Logging companies strip mountain slopes of their trees, exposing the soil to erosion.

An increasing amount of mountain land is dedicated to agriculture, such as this area in Bolivia.

AGRICULTURE AND TOURISM

Along with industries that extract natural resources from mountains, agriculture is spreading up mountain lands in less developed countries. Only about 14 percent of mountain land in North America is devoted to agriculture. But in Africa, almost half of mountain land is devoted to farming and grazing. The amount of agricultural mountain land in South America is nearly as high.

Changing agriculture

Mountain peoples have farmed and grazed animals for thousands of years. Many of the traditional farming practices were harmonious with mountain environments. In the foothills of Peru's Andes, for example, the mountainsides are covered with leveled sections called **agricultural terraces** that have been used for centuries to hold soil in place on steep slopes. Farming on terraces is an ancient method that helps stabilize soil against erosion. Higher up, on the Altiplano plateau, native peoples graze their llamas and alpacas.

In the past century, these traditional methods of farming have clashed with a changing world. As human populations increase, mountains become more crowded. In some places, people from the lowlands are pushed into the mountains when land is taken for development or for large, **commercial** farms. Scarce mountain land is exhausted by impoverished people who are forced to farm in areas unsuitable for growing or grazing. Many of these people need fuel as well as land and have cleared entire forests in their search for firewood. With forests gone, soil needed for farming is lost to erosion. The combined pressure from all these activities is pushing mountain land to the breaking point.

Tourism

Some damaging activities in mountain environments are caused by communities struggling to survive. But in **industrialized countries**, recreational activities are increasingly a problem on mountains. Tourism in parts of Europe and North America may threaten mountains more than such industries as mining and logging. According to BirdLife International, an international environmental organization, such bird species as the bearded vulture and golden eagle are being pushed out of the Alps and Pyrenees mountains by winter sports and summer tourism.

Tourism does not necessarily have to damage mountains. If not carefully planned, however, such facilities as ski runs and even mountain biking trails can damage slopes. Another problem is the spread of developments for vacation housing. Developments of second homes are an increasing part of the mountain landscape in the United States. They also cover vast tracts of land in the Alps of Italy, Germany, and Switzerland. Developments of this type require a large support system of facilities for waste disposal, water, and road access. Their environmental impact goes far beyond the housing developments themselves.

Even parts of the mountain world once considered remote are feeling the impact of tourism. Trash now litters the foothills around Mount Everest, a popular tourist destination.

Tourism is not necessarily harmful to mountains if proper steps are taken. It can be beneficial, creating an understanding of mountain environments on the part of visitors and providing income for mountain peoples. However, environmentalists stress that tourism development, like other uses of mountains, must be in harmony with nature.

Tourism and development, such as this ski resort in the French Alps, can threaten mountain habitats.

CLIMATE CHANGE AND MOUNTAIN GLACIERS

Earth's climate has always been changing. The history of the world's climate has been a cycle that gradually goes back and forth between warm periods and cool periods. However, many scientists warn that Earth is entering a period of **global warming** that is not part of a natural cycle.

Global warming is caused by the build-up of certain gases in the **atmosphere** that trap the sun's heat. This process is known as the **greenhouse effect.** The gases that trap the sun's heat are called **greenhouse gases.**

Most scientists agree that human activities, such as the burning of **fossil fuels** and the clearing of land, are the main cause of global warming. These activities release **carbon dioxide**, a greenhouse gas.

One notable sign of global warming is the shrinking of mountain glaciers. Snow and ice build up on high mountain peaks into glaciers and gradually melt, flowing down the slopes and eventually becoming rivers. But as Earth becomes warmer, the glaciers melt faster. This melting could cause problems for communities that rely on rivers flowing from mountain glaciers.

Kenya's Kilimanjaro rises in the distance above a tropical savanna landscape.

Snows of Kilimanjaro

Among the most spectacular sights in the world is the snow-covered peak of Kilimanjaro. But the snow coverage on Africa's highest mountain may not exist in 50 years. Some scientists warn that global warming will melt glaciers atop the 19,340-foot (5,895-meter) peak. They estimate that the ice fields on the mountain have decreased by 80 percent in the past century and are still shrinking fast.

Scientists are not completely sure that global warming is solely to blame for Kilimanjaro's shrinking glacier. Researchers from Austria and the United States measured the snow and ice atop Kilimanjaro for seven years, starting in 2000. During each year of the study, the icecap shrank by about 3 feet (1 meter). However, during 2006, a change in weather patterns brought heavy snow to the peak. Although the glaciers did not expand, they did become thicker. The study raises the question of whether rising temperatures or changes in precipitation are causing Kilimanjaro's snows to shrink. The culprit could be decreasing rainfall. Computer analysis shows these rains have decreased in recent years. At the same time, scientists suspect that global warming results in lower precipitation in the region.

Vanishing glaciers

Glaciers on other mountains are also decreasing. Since 1850, glaciers of Europe's Alps have lost up to 40 percent of their surface area. In a century, the glaciers of New Zealand's Southern Alps have decreased by 25 percent.

A 2009 study for China's Geological Survey Institute reported that the glaciers in China's interior are rapidly melting. As a result, dangerous flooding is destroying valuable cropland and pastureland, and forcing residents to leave. When the glaciers eventually disappear, the area will dry up and experience severe drought.

The mountains of the far western United States face a different problem. Soot and other contaminants from nearby communities are deposited on the snowpack. As global warming causes more and more snow to melt each year, polluted runoff increases. Purifying the water for drinking, farming, and fisheries has become more difficult and expensive. But, like in China, the real danger is that the snowpack will eventually disappear altogether and leave the area without any water at all.

Austria's Pasterze glacier, shown in 1875 (top) and 2004 (bottom), has shrunk dramatically due to climate change.

Endangered mountain gorillas live in cloud forests in Africa.

CLIMATE CHANGE AND MOUNTAIN LIFE

Environmental changes that heat up Earth's climate could cause drastic changes to mountain life, especially at high altitudes. Plants and animals adapted to cooler temperatures and other high-altitude climate conditions could be forced to higher slopes or even vanish if their surroundings become too warm.

Threatened cloud forests

The cloud forests on the upper slopes of many tropical mountains form an unusual environment. Not only are they watered by heavy rain, but they also absorb moisture from the misty clouds that cloak them. Water from clouds is especially important during seasonal decreases in rainfall. Many scientists who study cloud forests warn that a warming climate may disrupt the way in which these forests obtain moisture, eventually causing them to disappear.

For moisture to remain available, temperatures must stay cool enough for condensation to occur. A warming climate could push the clouds of condensation farther up the slopes, and the forests that remain behind would not survive.

Cloud forests, though small and scattered around the tropics, are havens of **biodiversity**. They are the homes of many rare animals, such as the mountain gorillas of Rwanda and Uganda in Africa. The cloud forests of Costa Rica are home to many rare frogs and toads. One of the most studied areas there is the Monteverde cloud forest. Since the 1980's, two-thirds of the species of frogs and toads that lived there seem to have vanished. One of them was the secretive golden toad, first seen in the 1960's. As far as anyone knows, it lived only there and is now thought to be extinct. Some scientists who have studied Monteverde say that the belt of clouds there is moving upward, possibly as a result of global warming.

Yellow-bellied marmots emerge from their burrows much earlier in the year due to climate change.

Shifting plants and animals

Other changes in plant and animal life are believed to be a result of global warming. Scientists have studied yellow-bellied marmots—rodents that resemble ground hogs—in one area of the Colorado Rockies since 1962. Today, the marmots emerge from their winter burrows in April, about a month earlier than when the study began. Since then, the average low temperature for April has risen almost 6 Fahrenheit degrees (3.3 Celsius degrees).

In several areas, mountain plant zones seem to be ascending the slopes. Studies in Europe's Alps show that plants are growing at higher elevations on mountainsides than they did in previous years. Trees that once grew only below alpine meadows of the Olympic Mountains in Washington have now edged above the old tree line. Plants of the alpine zone, above the tree line, are decreasing in some places. In parts of the Alps, the mosses and low wildflowers are being crowded toward the mountaintops.

The golden toad once lived only in Costa Rica's Monteverde cloud forest.

What Are Deserts?

Section Summary

Deserts are regions that have little rainfall and are often shaped by wind. Desert plants and animals have special adaptations to survive these tough living conditions.

Human activities threaten many desert plants and animals. Growing human populations near deserts strain limited water supplies. Mining, farming, and traffic from cars and recreational vehicles damage desert habitats.

Climate change may impact rainfall and water supplies, which could cause desert areas to expand. Spreading deserts would destroy existing ecosystems in the places they take over.

There is no generally accepted standard for what type of land qualifies as desert. According to some scientists, a desert is **The Valley of the Dinosaurs lies in Chile's Atacama Desert, the driest place on Earth.** a place that receives less than 10 inches (25 centimeters) of rainfall annually. Others define a desert as a region where the amount of water lost by **evaporation** each year is greater than the amount of **precipitation.**

Generally, however, a desert can be described as a barren region on Earth's surface that has little rainfall. By some estimates, such regions cover one-fifth of Earth's surface. Deserts in the United States span 500,000 square miles (1.3 million square kilometers). Australian deserts cover about 1 million square miles (2.6 million square kilometers), and the Sahara in Africa covers about 3.5 million square miles (9 million square kilometers).

The desert belts

Most deserts lie within two belts circling the globe, one in the Northern Hemisphere and the other in the Southern Hemisphere. Each belt is between the 15° and 35° **latitudes.** Between them is the equatorial region, which receives the most direct sunlight.

Hot air over the equator holds large amounts of water, which it releases when the air rises and cools. This is why the equatorial region has large rain forests. After the air releases its moisture, it sinks in the area of the desert belts. These areas are thus hot and dry, creating conditions in which deserts may form.

Kinds of deserts

Rain shadow deserts lie on the dry side of mountains. Most of the deserts in North America are rain shadow deserts, or at least partly so. The Thar Desert in India and the Ordos Desert of Central Asia are also rain shadow deserts.

Coastal deserts, such as Baja California in Mexico, generally lie on the western edge of continents near the Tropic of Cancer and the Tropic of Capricorn. The Atacama Desert in Chile, the driest place on Earth, is both a rain shadow and a coastal desert. The cool Pacific Ocean currents near its coast prevent water from evaporating to form rain clouds. Rain has not fallen on parts of the Atacama Desert for centuries.

Some of the most famous deserts belong to neither of the above categories. These deserts, sometimes called remote interior basins, are so far from a source of moisture that almost no water reaches them. Examples of remote interior basins include the Sahara of Africa and the Gobi of Asia.

Cold deserts

Some high-**altitude** deserts, especially those north of the desert belts, can be very cold in winter. These include the Gobi of Asia and the Great Basin of the United States. Winter temperatures in these deserts can drop well below freezing.

Many Arctic lands and much of Antarctica can be considered deserts. Although these areas are covered in snow and ice, very little snow actually falls there each year. In fact, the inland region of Antarctica is drier than most of the warm deserts on Earth.

Most deserts lie between the latitudes of 15° and 35° on each side of Earth's equator, such as the Sahara desert in northern Africa and the Australian desert in Australia.

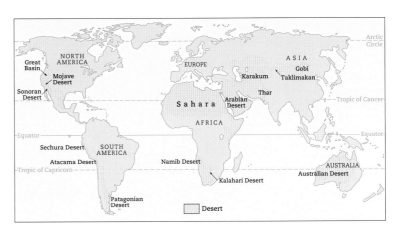

Fierce desert winds blow sharp particles of sand or dirt that carve out striking rock formations, such as this one in Egypt's White Desert.

DESERT CLIMATE

Deserts have a reputation as the hottest places on Earth. Some deserts are extremely hot. Temperatures in Death Valley, part of the Mojave Desert of California, have reached as high as 134 °F (57 °C). Normal daytime temperatures in the Sahara can easily surpass 100 °F (38 °C).

At night, however, even some hot deserts, such as the Sahara, can have temperatures below freezing. This is because dry air does not hold heat as well as moist air. After the sun sets in a desert, the day's heat quickly escapes. Thus, deserts are often environments with great extremes of weather.

Wind

Wind is one of the main forces that shape deserts. Wind wears away soft rock, such as sandstone, carving fantastic shapes. The wind blows huge amounts of sand into the air, carrying it for hundreds or even thousands of miles. Winds sometimes blow sand from the Sahara across the Atlantic Ocean to the east coast of the United States.

In desert regions with large amounts of sand, the wind can create dunes of various shapes. Crescent-shaped dunes called barchans form in areas where the wind blows from one direction. Long seif (*syf*) dunes with sharp crests form where the wind blows from different directions. Some deserts contain huge seas of sand, called ergs.

Rain

Occasionally, some deserts are pelted by sudden storms. Even during heavy bursts of rain, some of the moisture evaporates in the heat before reaching the ground. Desert soils allow water that does reach the ground to run off quickly, often through gullies where torrents develop in a flash. The water cuts through both sand and rock. The best example of this is the Grand Canyon in Arizona. The Colorado River, which originates in the Rocky Mountains, formed the canyon over millions of years by cutting through layers of limestone, sandstone, shale, and other rocks.

Where mountains rise above deserts, rain in the heights can also cause flash floods as water pours down the slopes into the desert below. Some deserts, such as those in the American Southwest, receive significant rain for a short season each year. The rain causes desert plants to burst into bloom, though they last only for a few weeks.

Sandstorms

One of the wildest types of weather in deserts is a sandstorm, a windstorm that carries a low cloud of sand through the air near the ground. Often, the cloud is less than 49 feet (15 meters) from the surface. The storm begins when wind rolls tiny grains of sand along the ground. As they pick up speed and bump into one another, they rise into the air. Once aloft, they can be whipped by the wind at speeds of more than 10 miles (16 kilometers) an hour. The storm ends when the wind speed decreases and sand falls to the ground again.

Sandstorms can be extremely dangerous. They reduce visibility to almost nothing and contaminate drinking water. People lost in sandstorms have perished. Blowing sand can also ruin machinery and electrical equipment.

Sandstorms consist of blowing grains of sand. They can reduce visibility to almost nothing.

Rainstorms are rare in deserts, but they can occur suddenly and cause flash floods.

The Joshua tree is an indicator plant of the Mojave Desert, which lies in the southwestern United States.

TYPES OF DESERTS

Like mountains, deserts are shaped by their distance from the equator and by their altitude. Both factors affect temperature, which in turn influences the type of life that characterizes a desert. The ways that latitude and altitude influence desert **habitats** can be seen in three deserts of the southwestern United States.

Sonoran Desert

The southernmost of these deserts, the Sonoran Desert, edges into Arizona and California from Mexico. It merges with the Mojave Desert to the north, which, in turn, meets the Great Basin Desert in south-central Nevada. In many parts of this area, mountains rise above the desert, some reaching to more than 14,000 feet (4,270 meters).

The Sonoran Desert is considered a hot desert. Summer temperatures average about 90 °F (32 °C) but often go well above 100 °F (38 °C). Winter temperatures average about 40 °F (4 °C) but during the day often reach above 70 °F (21 °C).

The true Sonoran Desert lies below 4,500 feet (1,370 meters) in altitude. A huge cactus called the giant saguaro grows between 2,000 and 4,500 feet (610 and 1,370 meters) in the desert. The saguaro is the tall, branching cactus often shown in films and other depictions of the American West. It is considered an **indicator plant** that is characteristic of the Sonoran Desert. The saguaro can live for more than a century, growing 60 feet (18 meters) tall and weighing more than 6 tons (5.4 metric tons).

Mojave Desert

North of the Sonoran, the Mojave Desert begins. It also has a large indicator plant, the 40-foot (12-meter) Joshua tree. The Joshua tree grows only at elevations above 3,000 feet (914 meters), where it sometimes forms large forests.

On average, the Mojave Desert sits at slightly higher elevations than the Sonoran. Because of its higher altitude and latitude, the Mojave Desert's average temperatures are somewhat lower than

those of the Sonoran Desert. However, one part of the Mojave Desert is one of the hottest and lowest places in the world—California's Death Valley. The Mojave Desert is considered a transition zone between the Sonoran Desert and the Great Basin. In the south, the conditions of the Mojave Desert are similar to those of the Sonoran Desert. The environment in the northern part of the Mojave Desert resembles the Great Basin.

Wildflowers bloom in Nevada's Great Basin, which has more vegetation than other deserts nearby.

Great Basin

The Great Basin, which covers most of Nevada and Utah and extends into western Colorado and southern Oregon, is a high desert. Large portions of this desert are above 4,000 feet (1,220 meters). Great Basin National Park in Nevada ranges in elevation from 5,000 feet (1,520 meters) to more than 13,000 feet (3,962 meters) above sea level. The highest levels of the region are above the tree line. Although summer temperatures can be as high as in deserts to the south, the Great Basin also may receive heavy snows in winter.

The Great Basin has more vegetation than other deserts in the region. The indicator plant for the Great Basin is the big sagebrush. Sagebrush areas are sometimes called desert scrub.

A CLOSER LOOK
Death Valley

Death Valley lies in the western part of the Mojave Desert, on the California-Nevada border. The lowest-lying place in the Western Hemisphere, 282 feet (86 meters) below sea level, is in Death Valley. This famed area is also one of the hottest spots on Earth. On July 15, 1972, a surface temperature of 201 °F (94 °C) was recorded there.

Death Valley is surrounded by mountains. Only about 2 inches (5 centimeters) of rain fall there in a year, but the wet, snow-covered peaks of the Sierra Nevada are within sight of the valley.

Death Valley

What Are Deserts? 29

DESERT PLANTS

The desert environment is harsh, with high temperature extremes, poor soil, and little water. Desert plants have adapted in many ways to these tough living conditions. To survive in a desert, a plant needs to find and use water efficiently.

Finding water

Desert surfaces are extremely dry, but some moisture from dew or other sources may be available. Many desert plants, such as the saguaro cactus, have roots that penetrate only a few inches or feet but spread out over a wide area. A mature saguaro can have a root system extending more than 50 feet (15 meters) around it. The network of roots enables the saguaro to take up water from a large area quickly, before it evaporates. It also helps the cactus cover a wide area in search of nutrients (nourishing substances), which are scarce in desert soil. Similar **adaptations** are found in the roots of many plants growing on mountains, where nutrients are also in short supply and water quickly runs off.

Other desert plants take the opposite approach to finding water. The mesquite tree and the creosote bush have roots that penetrate several feet or meters into the ground to find water stored below the surface. Sagebrush uses a natural suction pump to draw water from below. Pores in its leaves close, creating a vacuum that sucks water from the soil up through its roots.

Water conservation

Once a desert plant has obtained water, it must **conserve** it. Many desert plants, such as the acacia (*uh KAY shuh*), have tough leaves that are thick-skinned and waxy. This type of surface prevents water loss and protects against extreme temperatures. It is also found in many mountain plants.

The saguaro cactus can quickly absorb huge amounts of water, helping it survive in dry desert climates.

Many desert plants have adaptations that help them store a huge amount of water. Many cactuses, such as the saguaro and barrel cactus, have spongy interiors and pleated surfaces. When the interior tissues absorb water, they swell. The pleated surface of the cactus enables it to spread, making room for the expanding tissues. During a single heavy rain, a saguaro may absorb up to a ton (0.9 metric ton) of water. About 90 percent of a saguaro's weight is water.

A blaze of color

To save water and make the best use of nutrients, most desert plants grow slowly. Some desert plants spend almost all of their existence as seeds. They only sprout when the conditions are right. During the short rainy season, desert plants may bloom quickly in a blaze of colors. Within a few weeks, they sprout, flower, and reproduce—and then die.

Some desert plants live many years without blooming. It may take 20 years between blooms of the agave (*uh GAH vee*), a plant of North American deserts. The leaves of the agave form a low clump near the ground. When the agave blooms, its flower stalk shoots up from the center of the clump, sometimes at a rate of more than a foot (0.3 meter) a day. The stalks of large agaves can be twice the height of a tall man. After blooming, the stalk dies and the plant resumes its life as a low clump of leaves.

The agave blooms by growing a tall flower stalk from a clump of leaves.

The fennec fox hunts at night to keep cool. Its huge ears help it find prey.

The spadefoot toad burrows into the ground during dry spells to conserve moisture.

DESERT ANIMALS

Desert animals face many of the same challenges as plants in their effort to survive—extreme temperatures and scant moisture. Unlike plants, animals can move themselves around, which helps them find water and food.

Keeping cool

Deserts that look lifeless during the day can come alive at night, when it is cooler. Many desert animals stay under shelter during the heat of the day. Rats and mice, for example, remain in their burrows. Under the ground, the temperature stays several degrees below that of the surface temperature. The air is also more humid underground, as it is after dark.

Animals active at night have characteristics that help them function in the darkness. The fennec fox of the Sahara and Arabian deserts burrows by day and hunts by night. Its huge ears are an adaptation that helps it find prey after dark.

Mammals and birds have bodies that **regulate** their internal temperature, but a reptile's body temperature changes with its surroundings. Desert lizards control this potential problem by positioning their bodies so that they cool off or warm up as needed. Early in the morning, when the air is cool, a lizard can place itself at a right angle to the rays of the sun. In this position, it receives the most heat. As the temperature rises, the lizard can place itself head-on to the sun, so rays do not strike it as directly. In the heat of the day, the lizard may retreat underground or beneath a rock. Before night brings cool temperatures, the lizard may again bask at right angles to the sun.

Conserving water and food

Many desert animals, especially rodents, do not need to drink water. They get their moisture from the plants or prey that they eat. Kangaroo rats, which live in North American deserts, hardly ever drink water. The kidney of the kangaroo rat concentrates its urine to a form that is almost solid, thus conserving water. The lining of its nasal passages is designed in a way that cools the rat's breath, keeping moisture in when it exhales.

The bodies of some desert animals are able to store large amounts of food, allowing the animal to go for days or even weeks without eating. One of the best-known examples is the camel, which feeds on the toughest desert plants. Its hump contains fat deposits that nourish it when food is scarce. Some desert lizards store fat in their tails. The Gila monster, a poisonous North American lizard, is one such example. Its rounded tail resembles a club.

Explosive reproduction

The Great Basin spadefoot toad survives by using the same strategy as desert plants that bloom and reproduce in a short burst. The toads may spend months during long dry spells **dormant**, burrowed beneath the ground in an inactive state. When the rains finally come and water accumulates in temporary pools, the toads emerge. Vast numbers of them gather in the pools and mate. The tadpoles that hatch from the toad eggs become adults in a few weeks, before the pools dry.

The Gila monster, a poisonous lizard, stores fat in its large tail. It can live on this stored-up fat for months without eating.

HUMAN SETTLEMENT

More than 500 million people inhabit the world's deserts. But deserts also include some of the most untouched remaining wildernesses. According to a **United Nations** Environment Programme (UNEP) report, these wildernesses cover 60 percent of the world's deserts but will decrease to 30 percent by the year 2050. Among the threats cited by the report are climate change, high water demands, tourism, contamination of irrigated soils, establishment of military training areas, and the creation of **refugee** camps in war-torn areas.

Sprawling desert cities, such as Las Vegas, put pressure on limited water supplies in the area.

People pressures, water pressures

Overpopulation puts tremendous pressure on desert environments. Some people, such as the Bedouins (*BEHD u ihnz*) of the Middle East, have long lived in deserts. But as people become overcrowded in wetter climates, many people move into deserts, seeking land on which to graze their animals and build cities. These people require water and other resources to survive, threatening the already fragile desert **ecosystems.** Overpopulation may threaten the water supplies of entire countries, such as Chad, Iraq, Niger, and Syria.

In the southwestern United States, desert cities, such as Las Vegas, Nevada, and Phoenix, Arizona, have greatly expanded. Developments of thousands of homes have sprung up within a matter of months. Since the mid-1950's, the population of Phoenix has grown by more than 1.5 million people and the population of Las Vegas has grown by more than 500,000 people.

Together with agriculture, the increase in human population of deserts has placed a huge demand for water upon an environment where water is scarce. The impact of such demands is often felt far from the cities that create them. The Colorado River, which flows through desert for much of its course, has been dammed to produce drinking water and electric power for Arizona and

California. As a result, the **delta** where the river enters the Gulf of California is drying out and losing much of its **fertility**.

Low water, rising danger

Demands on **ground water** supplies have reduced the water table—the level of underground water—in deserts. Near Death Valley, in Nevada, the Devil's Hole pupfish lives only in a single pool within a limestone cave. These tiny fish spawn on a single rock shelf, which must remain below water. Ground water levels tapped by development east of Death Valley have threatened to lower the waters which the pupfish needs to survive. The pupfish have been protected by federal law but must be guarded carefully to prevent their extinction.

In many parts of the world, lowering the level of ground water under the desert has enabled salt water to creep in, threatening drinking water supplies. This is the case in several coastal areas of desert. In Libya, salt water has seeped several miles inland into desert ground water.

The Imperial Valley is one of the richest farming areas in the United States. The All-American Canal carries water to the region from the Imperial Reservoir, located near the Colorado River.

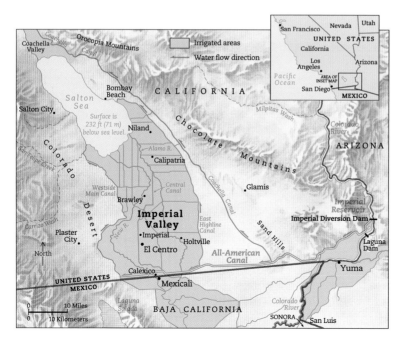

Future Uses of Deserts

Some scientists believe that deserts could provide conditions for certain types of agriculture that may benefit desert peoples without harming the environment. One of these pursuits is aquaculture, the farming of fish and other water organisms for food. A report from the United Nations Environment Programme says that sunlight and temperatures in such places as the Arizona desert and the Negev Desert of southern Israel could be ideal for farming fish and shrimp.

The sunny conditions of deserts could also make them ideal for solar power facilities, which capture energy from the sun to produce electric power.

Aquaculture facility in California

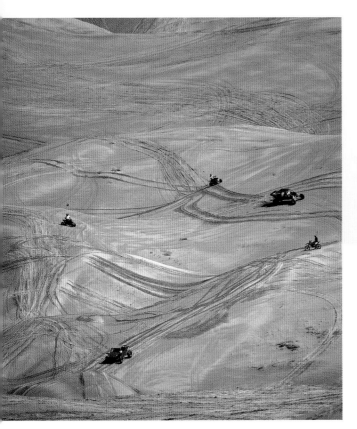

Unrestricted off-road vehicles can cause great damage to fragile desert ecosystems. Above, recreational vehicles scatter across California's Imperial Sand Dunes.

THE TRAFFIC THREAT

The camel is sometimes called the "ship of the desert." Indeed, for thousands of years, camels were the main form of transportation across the deserts of Asia and Africa. Today, railroads, cars, and other modern methods of transportation have replaced camels in deserts. Camels posed virtually no threat to the desert. But traffic from cars and recreational vehicles can harm desert ecology.

A fragile ecology

Some of the human activities that threaten deserts are not as damaging to other environments. The problem with the desert environment is that ecological balances in a harsh environment are easy to upset. Like the **alpine zone** of mountains, deserts take a long time to recover from damage. Plants that are destroyed grow so slowly that it may be dozens of years before they regain a foothold. In their absence, desert soil is vulnerable to **erosion** by wind and water. These plants can be harmed or destroyed by traffic in deserts.

The off-road question

For many years, a debate has raged about the use of recreational vehicles in the deserts of the United States. Some areas are off limits, but vast tracts of land are open to dirt bikes, dune buggies, and all-terrain vehicles. Tracks left by these vehicles, some several years old, scar many desert areas.

One of the areas hit hardest by recreational vehicle use is the Algodones Dunes, a sweeping area of sand that stretches 40 miles (64 kilometers) north from the Mexican border in Imperial County, California. It is one of the largest dune systems in the United States and the home of a handful of small animals and plants that live only there. Of the roughly 160,000 acres (64,750 hectares) of dunes, about 75,000 acres (30,350 hectares) are currently protected by the government. The rest is open to recreational vehicles, and **environmentalists** warn that the region could be forever damaged by this traffic.

Some environmentalists believe that recreational vehicles have no place in deserts. Others take a more moderate approach, seeking to restrict this form of recreation to designated areas. The debate has gone on for years and shows no sign of ending.

Traffic and development

On a worldwide scale, the amount of recreational traffic in deserts is dwarfed by transportation networks linked to development. Such activities as industry, mining, agriculture, and military training significantly change a desert environment. The roads and other **infrastructure** associated with these activities are at least as disruptive. Although many of these activities are necessary to modern civilization, the question is how to pursue these activities without turning deserts into true wastelands.

Heavy industry, such as this copper mine in the Atacama Desert in northern Chile, can significantly change desert environments.

The desert tortoise is threatened by human development in its desert home.

THREATS TO DESERT LIFE

Many plants and animals of the desert are declining or in danger of declining. The pressures on them vary. In years past, many large desert antelopes, such as the Arabian oryx (*AWR ihks*), fell victim to unrestricted hunting. Collectors have reduced the populations of some desert lizards, such as the chuckwalla of Mexico and the United States. They also have destroyed several types of plants for **commercial** trade, notably cactuses.

Laws have been passed to protect vulnerable desert species. Zoos have bred the oryx in captivity, and it has been released once more into the wild.

The desert tortoise

The desert tortoise of the Mojave and Sonoran deserts is particularly threatened. The tortoise, which can weigh up to 15 pounds (7 kilograms), is uniquely adapted to desert life. It has powerful limbs and long claws that it uses to burrow into desert soil during the heat of the day. During winter, the tortoise hibernates in a burrow until March, when the rains renew plant life. Desert tortoises get most of their water from the plants they eat, but they also dig shallow basins in hard soil to catch rainwater.

The International Union for Conservation of Nature classifies the desert tortoise as "vulnerable," which means that it faces a high risk of becoming extinct if left unprotected in the wild. A number of factors put the desert tortoise in danger. Roadways encourage the spread of nonnative plants. These, in turn, crowd out native plants, on which the tortoise depends for food, and aid the spread of wildfires. The tortoise is also threatened by drought, which can be intensified by human development. Ravens that prey on young tortoises have increased in numbers because they can obtain food from human sources, such as trash dumps. All of the pressures on tortoises make them more vulnerable to disease.

Forested mountains that rise above deserts are sometimes called "sky islands" because their environment differs so much from the dry lands around them. The plants and animals of these mountain areas are much different from those of the desert below. In some areas, such as the pine and oak forests of the Atlas Mountains that rise above the desert of Morocco, increasing development of industry, mining, and agriculture threatens the existence of sky island communities.

A "sky island" in Morocco's Atlas Mountains is home to plant life different from that of the desert below.

Since the 1980's, the federal government and scientists from conservation groups have been working on a program to prevent the tortoise from declining and to help its populations recover. It has been largely successful, but the tortoise is not yet truly safe.

Buffelgrass is a harmful nonnative species in Texas and Mexico.

Invader grass

Among the nonnative plants invading the home of the desert tortoise is buffelgrass. It was brought from Africa into southern Texas and Sonora, Mexico, as a crop for cattle to graze upon. It has spread through southern Arizona, where it crowds out native plants and adds fuel to wildfires.

Buffelgrass grows rapidly after a fire, so it can fuel fires more frequently and contribute to larger blazes. Even the giant saguaro cactus may be in danger if buffelgrass continues to spread.

CLIMATE CHANGE AND DESERTS

Global warming already may be affecting deserts. The overall temperature increase in deserts between the years 1976 and 2000 was more than the average global rise, according to a report by the United Nations Environment Programme (UNEP). The report warns that the temperature of some deserts will rise by more than 7 Fahrenheit degrees (3.9 Celsius degrees) by 2100. Climate change could also impact rainfall and water supplies, which establish the boundaries of desert areas.

Changing rainfall

According to the UNEP, precipitation in several deserts has changed significantly from 1976 to 2000. In the Kalahari Desert of southern Africa, rainfall has declined by 12 percent during this period. In the Great Salt Desert of Iran, it has declined by 16 percent.

The UNEP report warns that several deserts around the world will experience a decrease in rainfall of up to 20 percent by 2100. Deserts in the Southern Hemisphere, such as the Great Victoria Desert of Australia, will probably be most seriously affected. But the Great Basin Desert of the United States is another area that scientists believe is vulnerable to the effects of climate change.

Changes in rainfall and temperature will severely affect water supplies for people living in deserts, as well as people living in areas around them. Some desert plants and animals might not survive if their already low water supplies further decrease.

Mountains and the desert

The influence of climate change on mountains can be felt in deserts as well. Reduction in precipitation and rising temperatures that decrease the amount of mountain snow would mean less water for the desert below. Human beings, as well as desert plants and animals, would feel the results. A large amount of water used for agriculture and drinking water in such dry regions as the American Southwest, Central Asia, and the lower regions of South America's Andes comes from mountain snow. If the snow reservoir disappears, it would be like turning off the tap for people who depend on water from the heights. The United

Changing rainfall patterns can cause deserts to become even drier, destroying desert wildlife.

Nations Environment Programme warns that the teeming cities of the southwestern United States and Southwestern Asia would be the most seriously threatened.

Desertification

Climate change also threatens to extend existing deserts and create new ones in a process called **desertification.** Although deserts often support fascinating ecosystems, spreading deserts would destroy existing ecosystems in the places they take over. In addition, deserts cannot support nearly as much life as grasslands and other areas vulnerable to desertification.

Vast areas of sand dunes in deserts, such as the Kalahari of southern Africa, might be destabilized if the vegetation holding the sand in place dies. The dunes could spread, covering areas beyond the present desert. In many parts of the world, deserts are invading dry grasslands that border them. These grasslands are sometimes called semidesert or desert scrub. However, they are unique ecological communities. Once they turn to desert, they will no longer exist in their original state.

The Tuareg of Africa's Sahara desert rely on wells for their scarce water supplies.

What Are Grasslands?

Section Summary

Grasslands are open areas of grassy land that have few trees. Grasslands support large herds of big, grazing animals.

Uncontrolled hunting and warfare have damaged wildlife populations in many grassland areas. Other human activities have also damaged these habitats. These activities include farming, the development of cities and road systems, mining, and water diversion projects.

Global warming could turn many grasslands into desert. This change would threaten both the wildlife and people who live in these areas.

Grasslands are open areas of land that are dominated by grasses but have few trees. Deserts often merge into grasslands, especially when deserts lie in the **rain shadow** of mountains. As dry air passes over and then leaves desert regions, its load of moisture gradually is replaced. Eventually, enough of it forms that can fall as **precipitation** sufficient to support grasses.

Grasslands, such as these plains in central Mongolia, are open areas with few trees.

Grasslands cover the landscape in several parts of the world and appear at various **altitudes**, even on plateaus high in mountains. There are several varieties of grasslands, but most fall into two categories: **steppes**, with short grasses, and **prairies**, with tall grasses. Some scientists consider tropical **savannas**, grassy plains with scattered trees, such as those in East Africa, as a third category of grassland.

Formation of grasslands

Grasslands cover more than 14 million square miles (36 million square kilometers) of Earth's land. They exist on every continent except Antarctica. In North America and Asia, the largest grasslands are in the center of the continent. In Australia, grasslands lie around the edge of the continent, which has a central desert.

Like deserts, the amount of rainfall determines how a grassland forms. Usually, grasslands grow in places that receive between 10 and 40 inches (25 and 102 centimeters) of rain a year. Anything less often leads to a desert environment, and anything more is wet enough to support forests.

Grasslands compete against forests and deserts. During wet periods, trees invade grasslands. During dry times, they retreat. Meanwhile, deserts invade grasslands during dry periods and retreat when a wet climate rules. Strong grassland winds also wage war against trees by causing moisture to **evaporate.**

When grasslands are in a natural state, trees are kept in check by large grazing animals and wildfires. Before the prairies of the United States were settled, millions of bison roamed the plains. Fires triggered by lightning, or in some cases, Native Americans, occasionally roared over them. Although these fires destroyed trees, they were in many ways beneficial to grass plants. Seventy percent of the mass of grass plants lies under the surface in their roots and **rhizomes** (horizontal stems), an **adaptation** that allows them to recover quickly from fire. The fires also burned dead vegetation that can smother growing plants.

Few species, large numbers

Grasslands are full of life, but they don't support the large variety of life that forests do. Because grasses are dominant, the number of plants growing in grasslands is much fewer than that of forests. Grasslands have fewer animal species than forests, because the number of animals that can adapt to an area decreases along with the number of plants growing there. However, grasslands are so **fertile** that they can support vast numbers of animals, from tiny insects to large mammals. Natural grasslands can support huge herds of big, grazing animals.

Most grasslands lie between very dry lands, or deserts, and humid lands covered with forests.

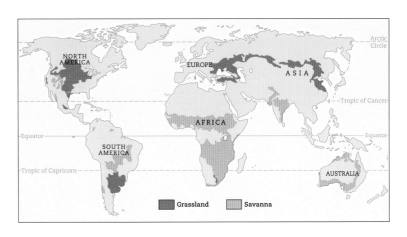

Shortgrass prairies, also called steppes, receive the least rainfall of all grasslands.

HOW RAINFALL SHAPES GRASSLANDS

The amount of rainfall in an area determines the type of plants that can grow there. Grasslands generally require more rainfall than a desert but less rainfall than a forest. The more rainfall a grassland has, the taller its grasses can grow.

North America's varied grasslands illustrate how rainfall affects a grassland's characteristics. The original grasslands of North America stretched from Illinois—with a few parts in Ohio and Indiana—all the way west to the Rocky Mountains, north into Canada, and south into Mexico, describing a region called the Great Plains. However, few natural grasslands remain in North America. Most of this region has been converted for agriculture, ranching, and other human activities.

North American steppes

The westernmost of North America's grasslands lie just past the eastern rain shadow of the Rocky Mountains and so receive less rain than other grasslands. Some scientists describe these grasslands as steppes. Another way to describe them is shortgrass prairies, because this region has the shortest grasses of the North American Great Plains. Grasses here are usually less than 1 foot (0.3 meter) high, and rainfall is below 20 inches (51 centimeters) a year. In some places, the rain total is low enough to approach that of a desert.

Mixed grass prairies

East of the steppes lies a type of North American grassland that is sometimes called mixed grass prairie. Here, between 20 and 30 inches (51 and 76 centimeters) of rain falls in a year, and the western short grasses mix with much taller grasses that grow on prairies to the east. This area lies in the western Dakotas, eastern Montana, northeastern Wyoming, and portions of Canada just to the north. Parts of this prairie also can be found in Nebraska, western Kansas, east-central Oklahoma, and central Texas.

Tallgrass prairies

The easternmost grasslands of North America are the tallgrass prairies. This area has some of the richest, deepest topsoil in the world. However, most of the tallgrass prairies have been destroyed to make room for farming and human settlement.

One of the reasons this region is so fertile is that it receives more than 30 inches (76 centimeters) of rain a year. Warm, moist air moving north from the Gulf of Mexico meets the cooler air from the west, creating weather fronts that produce significant rain. In some areas, there is enough rain to support forests, and grasslands merge with trees in the eastern edges of the prairies. But since Europeans settled the region, both grasses and trees have been replaced by farm crops.

Tallgrass prairie is the wettest kind of grassland and has rich, deep topsoil.

Pampas grass dominates the moister regions of South America's pampas, or plains.

GRASSLAND PLANTS

Though grasses dominate grassland vegetation, other plants grow in grasslands, too. They include a variety of colorful wildflowers. A few trees grow on grasslands called savannas. They are specially adapted to conditions that are drier than forests.

Grasses

There are almost 8,000 species of grasses. They range in size from about 1 inch (2.5 centimeters) tall to the heights of trees. Grasses have thick root systems that anchor them firmly into the ground. Much of the plant, in fact, is below the surface. Thus, grass can quickly regrow from grazing or even from fires.

Grasses spread in two ways. The first way is by seeds that develop from tiny flowers. The other way grasses spread is by rhizomes (surface or underground stems) that grow horizontally. The blades of a grass plant are its leaves, which absorb sunlight to use in **photosynthesis**, a process green plants use to make food.

Certain types of grass dominate particular grasslands, depending on geography and rainfall. Big bluestem grass is the dominant grass of unspoiled North American tallgrass prairie. It can grow to 10 feet (3 meters) high. Blue grama is a dominant grass of North American shortgrass prairie, or steppe. It usually grows no higher than 2 feet (0.6 meter). Pampas grass is a dominant tall grass of the South American pampas (plains), particularly the moister areas. A dominant species on the dry shortgrass plains of Tanzania's Serengeti is couchgrass, especially where other grasses have been heavily grazed.

Flowers

Temperate grasslands are splashed with colorful wildflowers during spring and early summer. Wildflowers of North American grasslands include prairie smoke, phlox, buttercups, Indian paintbrushes, and violets. In Russia's extensive grasslands, flow-

ers include peonies, tulips, and irises. Many of these flowers are wild versions of types cultivated for use in gardens. Wild tulips and poppies are especially common on some of the high-altitude steppes of Central Asia.

Colorful wildflowers bloom on a Midwestern prairie in the United States.

Trees

The most common trees on many of the savannas of East Africa are acacias (*uh KAY shuhs*). Some of these thorny trees are the size of shrubs, and others are taller than elephants and giraffes. There are about 1,200 species of acacias in the tropics and subtropics of the world. In addition to Africa's savannas, acacias also grow on many other grasslands throughout the world, including those in Australia and South America.

Scattered acacia trees grow on Africa's grasslands, providing food for giraffes.

Different species of acacia prefer slightly different **habitats**. Small whistling thorn acacias dot lowland savannas of East Africa. Their name comes from the whistling sound made by wind blowing through their branches. Red thorn acacia and gum acacia grow on higher ground. Large groves of mixed acacias grow around river courses that flow through the plains. The tall umbrella thorn acacia, with its great, spreading crown, is one of the most spectacular trees on the African savannas.

What Are Grasslands?   47

Prairie dogs are the most widespread burrowers of North America's grasslands.

Hawks hunt small grassland animals, picking them out from above with their sharp eyesight.

GRASSLAND ANIMALS

Grasslands support huge numbers of animals, both large and small. In addition to grazing mammals and the predators that eat them, grasslands are also home to many burrowing creatures that live underground, as well as various kinds of birds.

Burrowers

Most grassland burrowers are small or medium-sized. But Africa's aardvark (*AHRD vahrk*), which sleeps underground all day, is larger than most dogs. At night, it uses its huge front claws to rip open rock-hard termite mounds and then eats up the insects with its long tongue.

Prairie dogs are the most widespread burrowers on the grasslands of North America. Prairie dogs are small rodents that live in colonies, or "towns." Before the West was settled, some prairie dog towns were immense. One town in Texas covered 25,000 square miles (65,000 square kilometers) and was the home of 400 million prairie dogs. Their extensive burrows have nurseries, dens, turn-arounds, and escape hatches. Other burrowers, such as badgers and black-footed ferrets, prey on prairie dogs.

Birds

Prairie dogs also are hunted by hawks and other birds of prey. These far-ranging predatory birds thrive on grasslands. They are designed to cover long distances while hunting. They hunt by sight, with keen eyes able to pick out prey from high in the air.

Many smaller birds live on grasslands as well. Grasses provide a huge amount of seeds for seed-eating birds. Insects abound in the grass, providing food for birds that eat them.

Grazers

Grazing animals, such as horses and antelopes, thrive on grasslands. Many of these animals have special adaptations for grasslands, such as hoofed feet that enable them to run fast on hard ground.

Grazers also have special grass-eating teeth. Their front incisors are shaped like chisels for clipping grass, and their molars in the rear of their mouth grind up the grass to aid digestion. In Australia, kangaroos graze on grassland plants. Their teeth are similar to other grazers, such as horses.

Cheetahs, the fastest land animal, are well suited to running down prey on grasslands.

Large predators

African hunting dogs, coyotes, wolves, leopards, lions, and a host of other predators feed on the grazing animals of grasslands. The lion, sometimes called the "king of beasts," is one of the largest predators in grasslands.

Few predators are more suited to running down prey than the cheetah of the African and Asian plains. It is the only cat whose claws cannot be retracted. However, this is not a disadvantage for the cheetah. Its paw is doglike, and with its long legs it can outrun prey, such as antelope. The cheetah, which can run in bursts of speed up to 60 miles (97 kilometers) an hour, is the fastest land animal over short distances. But it can only run this fast over a few hundred yards or meters.

A CLOSER LOOK

Great Migrations

Huge herds of hoofed animals seasonally migrate across the grasslands. One of the best known of such migrations occurs each year on East Africa's Serengeti Plain. About 1.5 million wildebeests, plus more than a million other animals, such as antelopes and zebras, travel from the southern Serengeti in Tanzania to the Masaai Mara area of Kenya. Lions and other predators follow the vast herds of grazers.

Migration in the Serengeti Plain

What Are Grasslands? 49

HUNTING AND WARFARE

Grassland wildlife has been ravaged on many occasions by uncontrolled hunting, particularly of large animals, and by war. Often, the two threats are linked.

Human hunters

In the early 1800's, an estimated 20 million American bison roamed the grasslands of North America. By the late 1800's, only about 1,000 bison remained, almost all in captivity. American settlers slaughtered the bison for their hides and their tongues, which were considered a delicacy. The rest of their bodies was left to rot. The hunting was not **regulated** by any type of **wildlife management**.

Bison, once ranging across North America's grasslands, were nearly hunted to extinction in the 1800's.

Some historians claim there may have been another reason why the United States government allowed so many bison to be killed. The Plains Indian tribes depended on the bison for their way of life. Without the bison, the Indians were forced onto reservations. In this respect, the slaughter of bison was a weapon of war.

The sad story of the bison is now being repeated on the grasslands of Eurasia. Less than 20 years ago, 1 million saiga antelope roamed the grasslands stretching from Russia to Mongolia. Today, 95 percent of these antelopes have vanished. Saiga males have been slaughtered for their horns, an ingredient used in traditional Chinese medicine and thus worth large amounts of money. Some of them have also been killed to make room for livestock.

Today, the Wildlife Conservation Society, based at the Bronx Zoo, suggests that bison can be repopulated over large areas between Alaska and Mexico during the next century. **Conservation** groups are also working with the governments of Russia, Mongolia, and other countries in the region, in an effort to save the saiga antelope.

Other wars, other wildlife

Wars that have ravaged nations in Africa in recent years have also caused the decline of wildlife. Often, insurgents (rebels) and competing armies **poach** wildlife and sell products, such as elephant ivory, to finance their causes. Bands of defeated soldiers or displaced civilians sometimes kill animals for food. Among the animals that have suffered are elephants, gorillas, and antelope.

Warfare can increase the lethal effects of poaching in other ways as well. During and after wars, modern weapons, such as automatic rifles, fall into the hands of poachers who formerly relied on outdated firearms.

There are cases in which wars can benefit wildlife. The Demilitarized Zone between North Korea and South Korea, a "no-man's land" between the two hostile nations, has become a haven for rare bears, leopards, and perhaps even tigers.

Poachers hunt elephants for their tusks and leopards for their skin.

Antelope in Sudan

DEVELOPMENT

Like other natural areas, grasslands are undergoing development for a variety of human needs. These include housing and **urbanization**, mining, road systems, and water diversion projects. Some of the most threatened grasslands are dry plains at the margins of deserts. Expanding cities consume enough water to lower the water table beneath these grasslands, which could turn them into desert wastelands.

The spread of cities

Dry grasslands once covered 34 percent of Arizona's land before it was settled. Because of development, mainly from mining and the expansion of towns and cities, less than half remain today.

One victim of urbanization in Arizona is the burrowing owl. It is one of the smallest owls, weighing only 5 ounces (140 grams), and lives in burrows. The owls are declining largely because housing developments now cover the grasslands, pushing out the rodents that serve as their food source.

Conservationists, with the help of some developers, are trying to preserve habitats for the owls amid the spreading cities. In Arizona, a conservation group is even digging artificial burrows for the owls.

Urbanization and development have threatened grassland animals, such as the tiny burrowing owl.

Mining and industry

The high steppes of Central Asia are a vast, undeveloped region. Until recently, **nomad** herders were their main inhabitants. In the ground beneath these grasslands, however, lie oil, iron, copper, and other natural resources. Mining and drilling activities have moved into many parts of these grasslands, which had remained unchanged for thousands of years.

The grasslands of South Africa, which are rich in wildlife, are also rich in coal. South Africa is one of the top five countries in coal production. Although some coal is exported, the rest is used within the country, which relies on coal for more than 90 percent of its electric power. The processes used in mining coal strip vegetation from the land and can cause soil **erosion**. They can also pollute **ground water**, rivers, and lakes near the mining site. Conservationists have urged coal miners in South Africa to use methods that minimize damage to grasslands.

The soil over vast areas of the grasslands in the western United States has been stripped so that the coal beneath it can be mined. Some of these mines have pits hundreds of feet deep. Though some coal-mining operations have completely destroyed environments, others have tried to keep damage to a minimum and even repair the environments in a process called restoration. After mining, grasslands can be restored by refilling the mined area and replanting the surface with native grasslands plants.

Coal mines, such as this one in Wyoming, can destroy grassland environments.

Large concentrations of grazing cattle on farms can destroy grasslands.

AGRICULTURE

Human beings have long relied on
agriculture to supply food. However,
farming and ranching have been extremely destructive to the environment, and especially to grasslands.
Less than 10 percent of original North
American tallgrass prairie remains.
More than 71 percent of it has been
converted to agriculture. The Cerrado
savanna of Brazil, Paraguay, and Bolivia has seen a similar amount of agricultural development. Grasslands in
Africa are becoming more and more
developed as well.

Grazing

A natural grassland can support at
least 30 different species of large grazing animals. This is because different
animals focus on different plants and
eat in different ways. The damage they do to plant life is spread
around. Moreover, wild animals tend to wander. But when a large
number of a single type of livestock are concentrated in one area,
they can destroy a grassland. Certain livestock are especially destructive to grass. For example, sheep can chew grass down to
the roots, killing the plants. Domestic goats can pull up grass by
the roots.

Modern farming also competes with wild grazing animals in
the same area. Fences for livestock and crops cut off wild animals
from their migration routes, and sometimes even from their normal watering holes and feeding grounds.

In many less developed countries, growing numbers of
people have taken their livestock into dry grasslands that are
not suited to large numbers of domestic animals. The grazing
animals eat the vegetation holding the thin topsoil in place,
causing it to erode. The vegetation cannot recover, and eventually such places turn into wastelands in a process called **deserti-**

fication. Each year, an area the size of Texas becomes a new desert. Desertification is especially serious in southern Africa, the Middle East, central Asia, and northern China.

Farming

Many grasslands have rich soil and plenty of rain, and so are well suited for farming crops. But when grasslands are plowed for farming, the wild plants and animals that live there vanish. As human populations increase, more grasslands are converted to farms, destroying the native **ecosystems.**

In less developed countries, small farms are invading grasslands, but the threat to grasslands from large **commercial** farms is much greater. These farms usually plant **monocultures**—that is, only one kind of crop over huge areas of land. Although monocultures can efficiently produce food for humans, monoculture crops deplete the nutrients in the soil and often depend on chemical **fertilizers** to grow efficiently.

Because all of the plants in a monoculture are the same, pests that happen to feed on that particular kind of crop can multiply rapidly, requiring even more poisonous chemicals called **pesticides** to control them. Meanwhile, native wildlife that feed on seeds and insects in natural grasslands are forced out of monocultures.

Not all agricultural activity produces crops for food. Such crops as cotton are grown for their fibers. Other crops, including corn, are grown to be converted into **biofuel,** a plant-based alternative to oil-derived fuels. The use of biofuels may increase the amount of land that would need to be cleared in order to grow enough crops to meet food and fuel demands.

GREEN FACT

Scientists are working to develop biofuel from switchgrass, a tallgrass native to North American prairies. Switchgrass grows more quickly than corn, takes less land to grow, and requires fewer synthetic (human-made) chemicals.

Many complex, native grasslands have been replaced by monocultures on huge farms.

CLIMATE CHANGE AND GRASSLANDS

If **global warming** heats up Earth, scientists predict that many grasslands could turn into deserts. This change would not just harm the wildlife living in such areas—it would also harm people. Many grasslands in danger of desertification are now used for agriculture.

Changing weather

Grasslands are already subject to weather extremes. The prairies of the United States, for example, experience searing hot temperatures in summer and freezing cold conditions in winter. The **greenhouse effect**, the build-up of **carbon dioxide** in the **atmosphere** that is causing Earth's surface to warm, could make the climate even more extreme.

Climate change may cause the dry Gobi to expand into a neighboring grassland region in China.

Global warming could dramatically change the western prairies of Canada. In addition to higher temperatures the year around, precipitation patterns would change as well. More rain and snow would fall during winter and spring, but summer and fall would be drier, causing droughts to become more frequent. Today, sand dunes are scattered about the Canadian prairies, held in place by vegetation. A warming climate could kill the vegetation, causing these sand dunes to spread over the grasslands.

Global warming could also increase the temperature and change rainfall patterns in the lands between Texas and North Dakota. Such changes would significantly decrease the agricultural productivity of farms in those areas.

Invaders

Rising carbon dioxide levels could also cause certain plants to invade grasslands. For example, the fringed sage—a woody, inedible plant—thrives when carbon dioxide levels increase. Fringed sage is a tough plant that grows well up into the mountains. But once established in grasslands, it can quickly spread, out-competing native grasses.

A deadly cycle

Warming temperatures would also add to the impact of over-grazing on desertification. Many scientists predict that warming and overgrazing together will speed up desertification. Desertification could then intensify global warming, creating a deadly cycle. Plants help to control global warming by absorbing carbon dioxide from the air. But deserts cannot support nearly as much plant life as grasslands and forests. As deserts spread, less plants can grow and absorb carbon dioxide, which speeds global warming—in turn speeding desertification.

Uncertain outlook

While warming may turn some grasslands to desert, it also may change forests to grasslands. According to the National Wildlife Federation, forests and woodlands in eastern Nebraska could be replaced by grasslands if global warming continues.

Other studies have shown that certain grasslands might become wetter due to global warming. Experiments in California indicated that warming and a rise in carbon dioxide levels increased soil moisture by as much as 10 percent. Scientists are still trying to predict all the changes that global warming may cause.

Global warming may cause some forested regions to become grasslands.

Activities

ECO-ACTION

Protecting Earth's **ecosystems** starts with practices at home and in your community. Here are a few things you can do to help keep Earth green:

- Ask family and friends to join you in a cleanup day at a public park, beach, or forest preserve. Bring along enough trash bags and gloves for everyone who participates.

- Reduce your water waste. Turn off the faucet when cleaning dishes or brushing your teeth, and take quick showers.

- Work toward reducing your energy use. Simple ways to do this include unplugging electronic items when they are not in use, turning off unnecessary lights, and replacing standard light bulbs with energy-efficient ones, such as compact fluorescent light bulbs (CFL's).

- Reduce the amount of trash you throw out by switching to reusable items. Examples of ways to do so include purchasing reusable drink bottles and food containers, using cloth rags and napkins instead of disposable paper items, and printing on both sides of paper to reduce paper waste.

- Recycle metal, glass, paper, and plastic items to help save energy. Start a recycling program at school if one doesn't already exist.

- Instead of driving a car, walk, ride your bike, or take public transportation whenever possible.

Organize a cleanup day in your community.

ans and other items at home.

RESEARCH PROJECT: ENDANGERED SPECIES

Introduction

Endangered species are plants or animals that are threatened with extinction. Thousands of species of animals and plants are endangered, and the number increases each year. Conduct a research project to learn more about endangered species around the world or in your region.

Directions:

1. Research one of the following endangered species, or choose your own:
   - Elephants (Asian and African)
   - Gorillas
   - Chimpanzees
   - Bonobos
   - Giant pandas
   - Rhinos
   - Snow leopards
   - Tigers

   You can go to the following Web sites to look up information on endangered species:
   http://www.worldwildlife.org/species/item9135.html
   http://www.fws.gov/Endangered/media/spotlight.html

2. Ask your teacher or school or public librarian to help you find information on an endangered species. Together, come up with a list of things you would like to find out about this species. Examples of such questions include:
   - In which region of the world does this endangered species live?
   - When did this species become endangered?
   - What are past and present threats to this species?
   - How are people working to build back this species' populations?
   - What can governments and individuals do to help protect this species?

3. Create a report that gives important information about the endangered species. The report could be in the form of a booklet, poster, collage, blog, podcast, or a combination of media.

Glossary

adaptation a trait that helps an organism survive in its natural environment.

agricultural terrace a leveled section of a hilly area that has been cleared for agriculture.

alpine zone the level of a mountain above the tree line characterized by low, stunted vegetation.

Altiplano high, upland plains, especially those of Bolivia, Peru, and other countries of the Andes Mountains, reaching altitudes of more than 15,000 feet (4,572 meters) above sea level.

altitude height above sea level.

atmosphere the mixture of gases in contact with Earth's surface and extending far above.

biodiversity the amount of variety among plants, animals, and other organisms.

biofuel a liquid fuel made from plant matter, animal waste, or other biological sources.

botanist a scientist who studies plants.

carbon dioxide a colorless, odorless gas given off by burning and by animals breathing out.

clearcutting the removal of all the trees in a certain area of forest.

cloud forest a dense forest in tropical areas that is almost constantly covered by clouds.

commercial having to do with trade or business.

condense to make denser or more compact.

conserve; conservation to keep from harm or loss; the management, protection, and wise use of natural resources.

delta a deposit of earth and sand that collects at the mouths of some rivers and is usually three-sided.

desertification the process of turning into arid or desert land.

dormant a state in which bodily processes shut down so that little energy is used.

ecosystem a group of interrelated living things and the environment on which they depend.

environmentalist a person who wants to preserve nature and reduce pollution.

erosion the gradual wearing away of a material by wind, rain, ice, or other forces.

evaporate; evaporation to change from a liquid or solid into a vapor or gas; the act or process of changing a liquid or a solid into vapor.

fault a break in Earth's crust, with the mass of rock on one side of the break pushed up, down, or sideways.

fertile; fertility able to support growth; the bearing, or abundant bearing, of seeds, fruits, crops, or young.

fertilizer a substance that helps plants to grow.

foothills zone low, hilly area at the base of a mountain or mountain range.

fossil fuel underground deposits that were formed millions of years ago from the remains of plants and animals. Coal, oil, and natural gas are fossil fuels.

global warming the gradual warming of Earth's surface, believed to be caused by a build-up of greenhouse gases in the atmosphere.

greenhouse effect the process by which certain gases cause the Earth's atmosphere to warm.

greenhouse gas any gas that contributes to the greenhouse effect.

ground water water that pools underground in porous rocks.

habitat the place where an animal or plant naturally lives or grows.

hydroelectric developing electric power from water power.

indicator plant a plant that grows in a specific

area, which can help observers make assumptions about the habitat, such as its climate and soil type.

industrialized country a country where historical wealth and advanced development contribute to a relatively high standard of living.

infrastructure roads, bridges, buildings, and other public facilities.

lava hot, liquid rock from a volcanic eruption that has broken through Earth's surface.

latitude the distance north or south of the equator, measured in degrees.

leeward the side away from the wind.

lichen an organism consisting of an alga and a fungus, growing together on rocks, trees, or other surfaces.

magma the hot liquid material beneath Earth's crust from which igneous rock is formed.

molten made liquid by heat; melted.

monoculture the growth of only one kind of crop.

montane zone the level of a mountain at which mountain forests begin to dominate, often mixed with lowland vegetation.

mountaintop removal a mining practice where explosives are detonated on the tops of mountains in order to get to the coal or other material that lies beneath.

nomad a member of a tribe that moves from place to place.

pampas the vast, grassy plains of South America. The pampas are south of the forest-covered belt of the Amazon Basin, especially in Argentina.

pesticide a poison that kills pests such as insects.

photosynthesis the process by which plant cells make energy from sunlight.

plate tectonics a theory that Earth's crust is divided into a series of vast, platelike parts that move or drift as distinct land masses.

poach to illegally hunt wild animals.

prairie a large area of level or rolling land with grasses but few or no trees, especially such an area making up much of central North America.

precipitation rain, snow, sleet, ice, or hail.

rain shadow the region on the leeward side of mountains where rainfall is low.

refugee a person who flees war, disaster, or other problems for safety.

regulate to control by rule, principle, or system.

rhizome a rootlike stem lying on or underneath the ground, which usually sends out roots below and leafy shoots above. The rhizome stores food to be used by the new plant the following year.

savanna a kind of grassland with scattered trees and shrubs.

steppe one of the vast, level, treeless plains in southeastern Europe and in Asia.

subalpine zone the level of a mountain between the montane zone and alpine zone.

summit the highest point of a mountain or hill.

temperate not very hot, and not very cold.

tundra land with low vegetation above the tree line in the Arctic.

United Nations an international organization that works for world peace and human prosperity.

urbanization the spread of cities.

wildlife management the practice of maintaining wildlife at healthy levels with methods based on sound scientific principles.

windward the side exposed to the direction from which the wind is blowing.

Additional Resources

WEB SITES

Canadian Environmental Assessment Agency
http://www.ceaa-acee.gc.ca

Provides environmental assessments that contribute to well-informed decision making; supports sustainable development.

Encyclopedia of Earth
http://www.eoearth.org

Includes articles on a wide range of topics written by scholars, professionals, educators, and experts.

Environment Agency
http://www.environment-agency.gov.uk

Provides tools to make the environment a better place for you and for future generations; includes resources for schools.

EnviroLink
http://www.envirolink.org

A nonprofit organization that provides access to thousands of online environmental resources.

International Union for Conservation of Nature
http://www.iucn.org/

Works to find practical solutions to environmental and development challenges.

National Geographic
http://www.nationalgeographic.com

Provides information on environmental issues around the world; includes a student section.

Natural Resources Defense Council
http://www.nrdc.org

Contains the latest information on ways people are working toward environmentally friendly practices.

The Nature Conservancy
http://www.nature.org

Works to protect ecologically important lands and waters; includes an activities section.

United States Environmental Protection Agency
http://www.epa.gov

Many directions to go from homepage for information on the environment, including a student page.

World Wildlife Fund
http://www.worldwildlife.org

An organization that works to protect animals and ecosystems around the world.

BOOKS

The Down-to-Earth Guide to Global Warming by Laurie David and Cambria Gordon (Orchard Books, 2007)

Encyclopedia of Global Environmental Change (John Wiley & Sons Ltd., 2002)

Endangered Planet by David Burnie and Tony Juniper (Kingfisher, 2007)

This Is My Planet by Jan Thornhill (Maple Tree Press, 2007)

Index